Buzz, Hop, Zip!

Written by Samantha Montgomerie

Collins

This bug is quick.

six legs

3

This bug sings.

It hums songs.

This bug rubs its wings.

buzz

This bug hops.

Its long legs push.

This bug is in a web.

buzz

11

This bug has wings.

It zips off!

13

 Review: After reading

Use your assessment from hearing the children read to choose any GPCs, words or tricky words that need additional practice.

Read 1: Decoding

- Focus on words with the /ng/ sound and challenge the children to sound out and blend the following:
  sings   songs   wings   rings   pings   things
- Turn to page 2. Point to **quick** and challenge the children to sound out and blend. Can they identify the two pairs of letters that each make one sound? (*"qu", "ck"*)
- Look at the "I spy sounds" pages (14–15) together. Ask the children to describe what they can see. Next, take turns to find a word in the picture containing a /qu/or /z/ sound. (e.g. *queen, squirrel, zipper, buzz*)

Read 2: Prosody

- Model reading each page with expression to the children. After you have read each page, ask the children to have a go at reading with expression.
- On page 13, show the children how to read the sentence as an exclamation, using a tone of surprise.

Read 3: Comprehension

- For every question ask the children how they know the answer. Ask:
  - On pages 2 and 3, is this bug fast or slow? (*fast*)
  - On pages 6 and 7, what sound does this bug make? How does it make the sound? (*it makes a buzz noise; it rubs its wings to make the noise*)
  - On pages 8 and 9, do you think this bug's legs are strong? Why? (e.g. *yes because they push it into the air*)
  - Which bug do you think is the noisiest and why?